Writing that Works

Writing that Works

SHARON L. PYWELL

The Business Skills Express Series

BUSINESS ONE IRWIN/MIRROR PRESS
Burr Ridge, Illinois
New York, New York
Boston, Massachusetts

© RICHARD D. IRWIN, INC., 1994

Mirror Press: David R. Helmstadter
                                 Carla F. Tishler

Editor-in-Chief: Jeffrey A. Krames
Project editor: Stephanie M. Britt
Production manager: Diane Palmer
Designer: Jeanne M. Rivera
Art coordinator: Heather Burbridge
Compositor: TCSystems, Inc.
Typeface: 12/14 Criterion
Printer: Malloy Lithographing, Inc.

Library of Congress Cataloging-in-Publication Data

Pywell, Sharon L.
    Writing that works / Sharon L. Pywell.
        p.   cm.—(Business skills express)
    ISBN 1-55623-856-8
    1. Business writing.   I. Title.   II. Series.
    HF5718.3.P98   1994
    808'.06665—dc20   93-9288

Printed in the United States of America
1 2 3 4 5 6 7 8 9 0   ML   0 9 8 7 6 5 4 3

PREFACE

If you agonize over writing, this book is for you. Do you:

- Take twice as long to write something as you should?
- Know what you want to say but cannot put it on paper?
- Feel that writing has never been your favorite way to communicate?
- Prefer to pick up the telephone or drop by someone's office to communicate information?
- Believe that the documents you write don't get the results you want or expect?

Most people, even professional writers, find writing difficult. No one just *writes*. Writing is not simply getting something down on paper; it is part of a process of figuring out what you think. You must have a clear, complete grasp of your subject in order to express yourself clearly. Most of us dislike the painful truth revealed by the blank page: some contemplation or research must be done before we can honestly say, *I know just what I think*.

Rest assured, though; your writing skills can be strengthened. Clear, accessible techniques and exercises can improve your writing—this book deals with many of them. This book will give you:

- Specific techniques to organize ideas.
- Guidance to clean up fuzzy writing.
- Strategies to get you going again if you lose your train of thought or don't know where to begin.

- Methods to save time and organize your work habits.
- Ways to analyze your writing tone and content to help you get the responses you want from your readers.

In short, this practical book will give you concrete advice on becoming a stronger writer.

Sharon Pywell

ABOUT THE AUTHOR

Sharon L. Pywell, president of the Pywell Company in Boston, Massachusetts, specializes in assessing organizational needs and document development for strategic management planning, marketing, and fundraising. Her clients include the Boston Museum of Science, Head Start, Catholic Charities, WGBH, the Boston Public Schools, and Northeastern University. Ms. Pywell is an experienced teacher of business writing, marketing, and expository writing. She has won numerous awards for short stories, fiction, and creative writing; has written for professional publications and journals; and holds graduate degrees in writing and teaching.

ABOUT
BUSINESS ONE IRWIN

Business One Irwin is the nation's premier publisher of business books. As a Times Mirror company, we work closely with Times Mirror training organizations, including Zenger-Miller, Inc., Learning International, Inc., and Kaset International to serve the training needs of business and industry.

About the Business Skills Express Series

This expanding series of authoritative, concise, and fast-paced books delivers high quality training on key business topics at a remarkably affordable cost. The series will help managers, supevisors, and front line personnel in organizations of all sizes and types hone their business skills while enhancing job performance and career satisfaction.

Business Skills Express Books are ideal for employee seminars, independent self-study, on-the-job training, and classroom-based instruction. Express books are also convenient-to-use references at work.

CONTENTS

Self-Assessment

How do you feel about your current writing skills? This simple self-assessment will confirm your level of confidence, and suggest areas for improvement.

	Almost Always	Sometimes	Almost Never
1. I can complete a business letter that satisfies me in less than 30 minutes.	_____	_____	_____
2. I am confident that my sentences reflect a positive and clear tone.	_____	_____	_____
3. My business memos and letters generate the kinds of responses I seek.	_____	_____	_____
4. I can assess a letter or memo's clarity and organization in one quick overview.	_____	_____	_____
5. I use at least three techniques to write quickly and effectively.	_____	_____	_____
6. My paragraphs are limited to a single topic.	_____	_____	_____
7. I am experienced with several organizing strategies for memos, reports, and letters.	_____	_____	_____
8. I set important letters aside for a period of time before my final edit.	_____	_____	_____
9. My readers know what actions, if any, they are expected to take in response to my letters and memos.	_____	_____	_____
10. I know at least two methods of overcoming writer's block.	_____	_____	_____

1 | Defining Good Business Writing

This chapter will help you to:

- Keep your sentences brief and simple.
- Use a short word or phrase rather than a long one.
- Choose active verbs instead of passive ones.
- Assume a tone that conveys confidence in yourself and respect for your reader.
- Feel confident about what you are saying by knowing your facts well.

The difference between successful and unsuccessful writing lies almost entirely in clarity, or how clearly your ideas are presented. Clarity is actually the end product of several writing skills—good grammar, directness, brevity, specificity, and a confident tone.

If your sentences require two or three readings to be understood, your reader will be frustrated. All the persuasive data or language in the world will not convince your reader if he or she has decided that you cannot think.

Strong writing skills will help you accomplish your goals and build strong working relationships. They are one of business's most powerful tools.

Many people believe that conversational English and written English should be dramatically different. This belief is not necessarily well founded with respect to business English. A writing style that resembles a lecturing professor or an expert who uses five-syllable words will not make the writer seem more intelligent—it will frustrate readers and put a barrier between them and the writer. Good business writing does just the opposite.

It makes readers feel confident that they understand and can respond and contributes to smooth working relationships.

As you edit your sentences, imagine yourself speaking them out loud. Write as though you were talking directly to a person sitting across a table from you.

WHERE DO WE GO WRONG?

Why do intelligent, experienced people use unclear language? Some common reasons include:

1. **Being honestly misguided.** Most of us remember an English teacher who refused to allow any sentence to end with a preposition, even if that meant writing, "That is the kind of language up with I never shall put." Some teachers sincerely believe that heavy, academic styles are desirable. But as they say in the song, "It ain't necessarily so."
2. **Not giving the work enough time or attention.** Finding the shortest, simplest way to say something actually is harder than just rambling. Some writers need to set a complex letter or memo aside for hours or a day in order to edit it objectively a final time. Outlining, reading material aloud, and reworking—all are necessary components of fine writing that demand time and concentration, particularly if we do not write on a regular basis.
3. **Concealing weak material.** If people are unsure of themselves, they sometimes believe that drawing attention to the language instead of the ideas might hide badly thought-out ideas. This approach never works.
4. **Trying to avoid responsibility.** Some people use the passive voice to sidestep facts. When an administrator writes, "The invoices appear to have missed their filing date," she or he is using the passive voice to avoid naming the person who made the error and describing how the error was made.

What price do we pay for ignorance, inattention, anxiety, and evasion?

Inattention and ignorance. The writer who uses muddy or inaccessible language also appears muddy and inaccessible. In many work situations, what we write makes the most lasting impression on our colleagues, and they will judge us accordingly.

Anxiety. Some readers will quickly see that anxious writers do not understand their subject and other readers simply will be put off by the writing's complexity.

Evasion. The department or organization that cannot honestly address its errors never will be able to correct them.

KEEP YOUR SENTENCES BRIEF AND SIMPLE

Keep your sentences brief and simple, even if you must chop a long sentence into two or more shorter ones. As a rule of thumb, *put one idea in one sentence.* Like most good rules, this is not hard and fast. Sentences should vary in length and rhythm. Your goal is not to turn out rapid-fire, homogeneous little sentences, but to stick to what you need to say and go no further.

Here is an example of a sentence that lost its way when it tried to move in two directions at once:

With regard to all the aforementioned problems about getting to work stations long after the standard time, the supervisors recommend staggering shifts, and they do not want to use formal reprimands as part of the solution process right now.

The writer here discusses two subjects, lateness and disciplinary action, in one sentence. The end effect reduces each point's impact.

A more effective version of this sentence might read:

The supervisors recommend staggering shifts to reduce tardy arrivals at work stations. They feel that formal reprimands are not the best immediate solution to the problem.

■ Exercise 1

Rewrite the following sentences, restructuring them for clarity.

1. Janice wants to cut down on time spent managing telemarketers and thinks that they aren't evaluated often enough.

_____

_____

_____

2. I do not believe that the equipment was shipped on time and the invoicing was not even coordinated with the ordering process.

_____

_____

_____

Sample solutions appear on page 73.

USE A SHORT WORD OR PHRASE RATHER THAN A LONG ONE

Most of us have received a memo at some time containing a sentence like this one written by a superintendent of schools:

In the spirit of collegiality with commitment toward maximizing faculty involvement in the exploration and resolution of issues and needs confronting this Division in response to its multidimensional challenges, I suggest that the departments target representatives to begin the divisional identification of the issues and needs considered most relevant to determine what formats would be most convenient.

Perhaps the coldest way to assess this sentence is to ask five impartial readers to describe the author's character. Adjectives like evasive and confused might be named, among others. Simplicity and a direct tone convey intelligence and respect for the reader. Muddy writing conveys just the opposite.

Compare the original sentence with the following rewrite:

Each Department will elect teachers to represent them in the faculty committees responsible for developing our final systemwide curriculum.

If you received two memos, each containing one version of the superintendent's sentence, which version would generate a positive response?

■ E x e r c i s e   2

Rewrite the following sentences to make them clearer.

1. Pursuant to the rules being reexamined as of this date by the administration in charge of Human Resources, endeavor to employ uncomplicated words in writing.

_____

_____

2. The occurrence of the accident took place in the area around which we were spending our afternoon in the park closest to Route 5.

_____

3. What I have done is read every one of the memos in question and pulled all of the ones that I think we should have the lawyers look at.

_____

4. Utilization of part-time secretarial personnel will make possible the finalization of the report within the allowable time frame.

_____

5. The expenditure for the purchase of this computer was over 1,000 dollars.

_____

6. I made the recommendation that we effect the redistribution of the management of accounts until after our next meeting.

_____
_____

Sample solutions appear on page 73.

Brevity and a Direct Voice

Often we use an unnecessarily long or antiquated word when a clear word or short phrase would be better. Here are some simple alternatives to needlessly formal words and phrases:

Instead of	Use
commence	begin
nevertheless	but
terminate	end
advise	tell
despite the fact that	although or though
succeed in making	make
give consideration to	consider
have need for	need
we would like to ask that	please

■ E x e r c i s e   3

Opposite each word or phrase below, write a word or phrase that says the same thing more clearly.

Wordy or Complex	Clearer
at the present time	_____
due to the fact that	_____
in order that	_____
with regard to	_____
utilize	_____
visualize	_____
in the near future	_____
ascertain	_____
concur	_____
facilitate	_____
endeavor (as a verb)	_____
in close proximity	_____
in view of the fact that	_____

Sample solutions appear on page 73.

WRITE IN THE ACTIVE VOICE

"Active" voice refers to sentence structure focusing on a force acting upon an object or situation. "Passive" voice refers to sentence structure focusing on an object or situation being acted upon by a force. The following examples demonstrate the difference between active and passive voice.

Active Voice

The manager *restructured* the compensation package and *made* bonuses possible.

The batter *hit* a home run.

Passive Voice

Bonuses *were made possible* when the compensation package *was restructured* by the manager.

A home run *was hit* by the batter.

There are several reasons to choose the active voice. The writer who uses passive voice may convey a sense of powerlessness. In business writing, the passive voice often appears when morale is low or the writer feels insecure. These negative feelings are conveyed to the readers.

The passive voice also communicates an unwillingness to be direct. "The reports must be filed by Tuesday" is not as clear as "You must file the reports by Tuesday." "Quarterly goals were not met" does not put the subject in as clear view as "The sales department did not meet quarterly goals." In business writing, the clear view is always the best view.

■ Exercise 4

Rewrite these sentences, replacing the passive voice with an active voice. Make the language more direct.

1. The statement of the problem was set forth by the division director.

_____

_____

2. Avoidance of the problem should be sought.

_____

_____

3. It has been suggested that a review board be established by the finance department to oversee cash flow.

_____

_____

4. It is believed that an increase in sales over the last quarter would make bonuses a possibility this year.

_____

_____

5. Assignments were made without regard for the employee's previous experience and existing responsibilities.

_____

_____

Sample solutions appear on page 74.

ASSUME A TONE THAT CONVEYS CONFIDENCE AND RESPECT

John Vogel, a computer hardware distributor, called Donna Vega, his warehouse manager, into the main office to let off some steam. "You're holding too much stock on the floor and new orders are getting backed up in expensive storage! It's a sign of poor management and I'm not happy with the situation. So do something, fast," he ordered.

Anxious to show a quick response, Donna went back to her desk and reviewed the problem. She found several instances where buyers had not made decisions about how to get equipment delivered or had delivery held up because of payment issues. She fired off several letters, each containing this sentence: "We cannot hold your equipment any longer than two weeks for any reason, or storage charges will be added to your bill."

After reading this sentence, customers had several reactions, none of them pleasant: they became nervous, angry, and irritated. Customers swamped Donna with telephone calls trying to arrange delivery, giving excuses, or protesting the sudden demand that they act. In the end, almost every customer was rattled and unhappy. ■

An environmental control agency was given the job of publicizing federal standards for acceptable levels of pollutants in waste runoff. The director of the agency, Craig

Nussbaum, wrote to every corporation and agency that might remotely have been involved in waste disposal. His letters contained this sentence: "Your corporation's failure to adhere to the federal standards of waste disposal will result in significant fines."

As soon as the letters reached their destinations, Craig started receiving disgruntled calls. "What makes you think *we* are polluting?" one caller demanded. "How dare you threaten us?" said another.

Craig was shocked. "I was only giving the facts," he said. ∎

How could Donna and Craig have generated support and cooperation rather than anxiety and irritation? Their sentences were grammatically correct and their messages were clear. Still, their letters failed because they did not generate the responses Donna and Craig wanted.

Put yourself in the position of the person reading Donna's letter. If you had read, "We will be happy to hold your equipment for you for another two weeks without any storage charge and expect that you will be able to arrange its removal by then," you might have picked up the telephone and asked the distributor to add delivery service to your bill. You probably would not have responded to the letter with a complaint.

If you had read in Craig's letter, "We have been selected as the local agency responsible for helping you understand federal pollution standards and controls," you probably would not have become defensive and angry. You would have seen Craig as someone helping rather than threatening you. Offers of help typically do not provoke defensive or angry reactions.

Mirroring

If you listen carefully to conversations around you, you will find that negative complaints often receive negative responses; aggressive threats often receive aggressive defenses. This pattern is called *mirroring.* You can use this pattern to your advantage because it works as effectively in the reverse. Positive tones generally solicit positive responses. Faith and goodwill generate confident cooperation.

Always imagine yourself in the position of the person reading your report, letter, or memo. If you seek the reader's respect and competence, make sure you demonstrate respect and competence yourself.

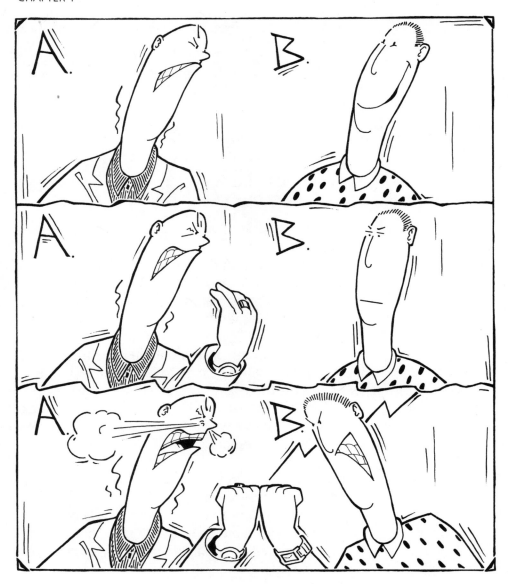

Exercise 5

Rewrite the following sentences to make them more positive. Use a tone that you want your readers to mirror.

1. If your department continues to fail to meet deadlines, action will be taken.

_____

_____

2. We never take telephone orders on weekends.

_____

_____

3. No one will pay more than $150 for this product.

_____

_____

4. Customer complaints tie us up all day, and normal ongoing work cannot be done.

_____

_____

5. If I had received more timely advice and assistance, the errors would not have been made.

_____

_____

Sample solutions appear on page 74.

KNOW YOUR FACTS WELL ENOUGH TO FEEL CONFIDENT ABOUT YOUR MESSAGE

If your work is presented concisely and directly, you've won half the battle. When your writing is clear, you appear knowledgeable and assured. Most of us listen to a confident voice without reservation. But the flip side is also true: We do not rely on information that comes from someone whose writing is evasive or muddy. Writing characteristics that convey knowledge are:

- Specificity.
- Accuracy.
- Economy.

Specificity

Writers must use specific images, situations, and data to convey a level of knowledge about any subject. "I feel that being generous is an important characteristic" doesn't convey as clear a picture of the speaker as "I give a dollar to every homeless person on the street I pass."

Describing generosity as an important characteristic is vague and theoretical and could have been written by anyone considering the subject. The image of an outstretched hand with a bill shows specific facts and events.

Ask three people from different backgrounds to define the word "far" and see what happens. To a Manhattanite, "far" might be 1 mile. To a Montana rancher, it might be 100. To a businessperson who travels internationally four times a month, it might be 5,000 miles.

We risk a great deal when we are not specific. We appear to be less thoughtful and less informed, and we jeopardize the reader's faith in us. When we are not specific, we confuse our readers and often get unexpected or unwanted responses.

Accuracy

Accuracy is critical to gaining our reader's respect and cooperation. If a reader spots one inaccurate fact in a report, he or she will question every other fact in the report. Professional reputations are built making sure your facts are right. Consistent accuracy inspires trust. It is well worth the time it takes to check facts as well as edit for style and grammar.

Economy

Rambling or saying more than is necessary gives your reader the impression that you do not know your subject. Saying one word more than you need to is saying too much. Look at the following letter.

Harvey Diaz has a real problem and a valid complaint. Is he helping Cassandra Epstein to solve his problem? What is his invoice identification number, so she can quickly locate an invoice? What kind of alarm system did he purchase? What day was it purchased? When was it installed? Did it come with a warranty?

Consider the questions that Cassandra might ask herself as she read Harvey's letter and tried to respond. Think of her frame of mind and willingness to come to Harvey's aid in the face of a threat to file complaints, particularly when his language implies that she is personally responsible for his problem.

January 12, 1993

Ms. Cassandra Epstein
Johnson Alarm Company
36th North Avenue
Natick, MA 02368

Dear Ms. Epstein:

Last winter we bought some alarms from your company and we've been having trouble with them. As you know, security is an important issue here and walking around feeling like the system just doesn't work puts our security people all under a constant, irritating strain.

The alarm goes off for no apparent reason and it's gotten to the point where the staff just ignore it. I don't know if it would work if we actually were burglarized because it hasn't happened yet, but it certainly works when we accidentally trip the system on our way to lunch.

If you can't do something about it quickly we will consider going to the Better Business Bureau to register a complaint.

Sincerely,

Harvey Diaz

Two telephone calls, another exchange of letters, and three weeks later, Cassandra finally gets enough information to determine what kind of system and warranty Harvey has and how much the repair will cost. Ultimately, Harvey's problem is resolved. Think of the time, energy, and aggravation that would have been saved had Harvey been specific and courteous in the first place.

■ **E x e r c i s e   6**

Rewrite Harvey's letter in the space below, deleting unnecessary language, altering tone, and including helpful specifics that make it a more successful business document.

_____
_____
_____
_____
_____
_____
_____
_____
_____
_____
_____
_____
_____
_____
_____
_____
_____
_____
_____
_____
_____
_____
_____
_____
_____
_____
_____
_____
_____
_____

Sample solutions appear on pages 74 and 75.

Chapter Checkpoints

Writing for Clarity

✓ When in doubt, use short, to-the-point sentences.

✓ Choose active verbs.

✓ Avoid passive verbs whenever possible.

✓ Let the tone of your message underline your self-confidence.

✓ Ensure that your respect for the reader comes through.

✓ Know your facts before writing.

2 | Paragraphs that Work

This chapter will help you to:

- Keep paragraphs unified.
- Control paragraph length.
- Position a topic sentence effectively.
- Build transitions between paragraphs.

Paragraphs make your thoughts more accessible to readers. They break your entire document—whether it be a letter, memo, report, or proposal—into blocks of related sentences. This makes it easier for you and your reader to predict what's coming, to find what you're looking for, and to get main points by skimming.

WHAT'S A PARAGRAPH?

A paragraph is a group of sentences related to one another by a single idea or subject. Just as every word in a sentence must be necessary, so every sentence in a paragraph must serve a purpose.

A simple rule about paragraphs is: one paragraph, one idea. The most common mistake writers make is putting too much into one paragraph.

Paragraphs organize material and control the visual impact of the page. Pages of text with no breaks or white space tire the reader's eye. Breaking the same words into tightly conceived paragraphs will create a more inviting page that is easier to understand.

Look quickly at the following letters.

2

Hurricane Dance Company
One Park Square
Cambridge, MA 02138

June 13, 1993

Paula Anderson, Dance Coordinator
National Endowment for the Arts
1330 Connecticut Ave., SW
Washington, DC 20003

Dear Paula:

We write to notify you of a change in plans for one of the key players in the Hurricane Dance Company program you funded this year. Last year, when we were putting together our program for 1994–95, we asked John Ellery to choreograph a new dance specifically for our company. When he said yes, we proceeded to draft the proposal to the National Endowment asking for financial support for that project. Upon hearing of our award, we contacted Johnny to confirm dates for his first visit. We learned that he is no longer available to set the work. His manager arranged a very lucrative tour for him in Europe; he is unavailable until 1995. We now have the choice of waiting for his return or finding a new choreographer. We feel that the company needs a new dance for its upcoming season, and we believe that a work by Elaine Massey would meet our artistic needs as well as one by Johnny. We write to ask if we can simply use the funds you awarded us for Johnny's work and apply them to another dance. We believe that the award was made in the spirit of furthering the Hurricane Dance Company's repertoire rather than furthering Johnny's career, so you will not mind the switch. As you know, the $15,000 award included travel for him and two members of his company back and forth from New York five times during the period he worked with us, and a fee for permanent rights to the dance. It also included the standard costs of costume designers, lighting designers, our own dancers' time, an accompanist, and production costs for its first performance. We have discussed the particulars of the budget with Elaine and she feels she could contain costs to directly match the existing budget, so no new funds would be needed. We appreciate the NEA's flexibility and commitment to the development of individual dance company repertoires, and hope you will agree to this change. A reply before the end of July would make it possible for Elaine to make the necessary shifts in her schedule. Thank you for your time and attention.

Sincerely,

Peter Santiago
General Manager, Hurricane Dance Company

The two letters convey virtually the same information, though the second letter contains fewer sentences. After reading both letters, which letter communicates more clearly?

LENGTH

Paragraphs can be 2 or 3 or 20 sentences long. In business writing, try to keep paragraphs brief. Short paragraphs make documents look accessi-

Hurricane Dance Company
One Park Square
Cambridge, MA 02138

June 13, 1993

Paula Anderson, Dance Coordinator
National Endowment for the Arts
1330 Connecticut Ave., SW
Washington, DC 20003

Dear Paula:

We write to notify you of a change in plans for one of the key players in the Hurricane Dance Company program you funded this year.

Last year, when we were putting together our program for 1994–95, we asked John Ellery to choreograph a new dance specifically for our company. When he said yes, we proceeded to draft the proposal to the National Endowment asking for financial support for that project. Upon hearing of our award, we contacted Johnny to confirm dates for his first visit. We learned that he is no longer available to set the work. His manager arranged a very lucrative tour for him in Europe; he is unavailable until 1995.

We now have the choice of waiting for his return or finding a new choreographer. We feel that the company needs a new dance for its upcoming season, and we believe that a work by Elaine Massey would meet our artistic needs as well as one by Johnny.

We write to ask if we can simply use the funds you awarded us for Johnny's work and apply them to another dance.

We believe that the award was made in the spirit of furthering the Hurricane Dance Company's repertoire rather than furthering Johnny's career, so you will not mind the switch.

We have discussed the particulars of the budget with Elaine and she feels she could contain costs to directly match the existing budget, so no new funds would be needed.

We appreciate the NEA's flexibility and commitment to the development of individual dance company repertoires, and hope you will agree to this change.

A reply before the end of July would enable Elaine to make the necessary shifts in her schedule. Thank you for your time and attention.

Sincerely,

Peter Santiago
General Manager, Hurricane Dance Company

ble and well-organized. They make it possible to scan an entire document quickly and find the information you need.

When choosing between a shorter and a longer paragraph, choose the shorter one. Don't be afraid of white space on the page.

2

Exercise 1

Strengthen the following paragraph. Cut out all sentences that do not contribute to its meaning, then break it into shorter paragraphs.

I think that everyone needs an old-fashioned wife. Nothing is more comforting than walking in the door at the end of a long day and smelling a home-cooked meal in the oven. Everyone needs someone to set up their social calendar and get the car to the mechanic when it's on the fritz. I hate dealing with mechanics. I'm not real social. Most people aren't. Good wives are. Good old-fashioned wives listen attentively to your stories, don't bore you with complaints about being a good old-fashioned wife, and raise children so polite and good-hearted that they let you eat dinner uninterrupted. If they work, they still get that dinner in the oven by the time you reach the door, and they hold jobs that let them stay home with the kids if they're sick and get there late because they had to get the car to the garage. You remember how I feel about mechanics. To sum up, if my husband would let me get married, I'd go looking for one tomorrow, but he's against it. So—I remain wifeless.

_____
_____
_____
_____
_____
_____
_____
_____
_____
_____
_____
_____
_____
_____
_____
_____
_____

Sample solution appears on page 75.

THE TOPIC SENTENCE

In a paragraph, the topic sentence presents the main idea.

Every sentence in the following paragraph supports the statement made in the topic sentence (in bold type).

Finally, after two years of effort, I fulfilled my dream of seeing the lake at sunset. This was harder to accomplish than you might think because sunset is the time of day when my children are most demanding. After months of painting glorious pictures of all the amusements found on lakes at sunset, I convinced my children to cooperate. I got my wish and drove off at last, hoping their good humor would last through the adventure.

Topic sentences do not have to appear at the beginning of a paragraph, though readers typically look for them there. Here is an example of how the paragraph above could be restructured to shift the topic sentence's position:

My children resisted me right down the line. I struggled to move them, but late afternoon was their most demanding and least cooperative time of day. For months I painted glorious pictures of all the amusements found on the lake at sunset, and at long last my children got in the car and promised to humor me. **Finally, after two years of effort, I fulfilled my dream of seeing the lake at sunset.**

Think of paragraphs as having shapes, with the topic sentence appearing at the most focused part.

Common Paragraph Designs

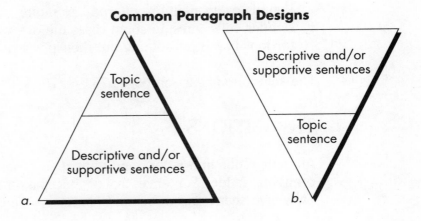

■ E x e r c i s e   2

Below you will find four paragraphs. Underline the topic sentence of each one.

1. All the frustrations of Andy's day left him feeling short-tempered and anxious. The moment he arrived at work, he discovered three errors in the night shift's work. Worse, the errors attracted a great deal of attention because Andy's own boss chose this particular day

to drop in and review the morning shipping schedule. Not only did everything seem to go wrong, but everyone in the world seemed to be watching it happen.

2. The best way to handle paperwork is to touch each document that crosses your desk only once. If a document is highly important, telephone, write, or dictate a response immediately. If it is moderately important, dash off a reply directly on the letter or memo itself, or redirect it to an appropriate person. If you believe it could wait, let it wait—forever. Toss it in a special drawer that holds things you never expect to do. This is the most efficient use of your time.

3. You can be someone who works methodically, never leaving any detail to rest until your work seems perfect. You can be sweepingly quick, happier accomplishing a great deal than one perfect thing. You can be a dreamer who is concerned with nothing at all but what is in your head at any given moment. You can succeed no matter what kind of person you are, if only you find a life's work that fits your character.

4. People typically do not think of prejudice in the workplace as something that extends to those with weight problems, but it does. We know that women, the disabled, and minorities suffer job discrimination. It is also true that individuals who are more than 20 pounds overweight are offered less money to do the same job as slender colleagues; in some cases the overweight are even rejected for jobs based on nothing but their physical appearance.

The solution appears on pages 75 and 76.

TRANSITIONS

All paragraphs in a letter, memo, or report must be linked together like rungs on a ladder. Sentences that connect paragraphs are called *transitions*. They give shape and direction to letters, memos, and reports.

The following illustration shows paragraphs of a letter requesting that a company reexamine its leave policies. Transition sentences that link the paragraphs are suggested.

> The first paragraph makes a request that the company consider dividing a management job into two part-time positions.

Transition sentence to second paragraph: Consider these three reasons for this kind of job reconstruction.

> The second paragraph offers a good reason for considering this kind of job reconstruction, citing a research study indicating that part-time people working half-time accomplish 89 percent of what full-timers accomplish. The paragraph goes on to offer examples supporting the research findings.

Transition sentence to third paragraph: Besides productivity, employee levels of job satisfaction were higher.

> The third paragraph describes how job satisfaction positively impacts the quality of people's work.

Transition sentence to fourth paragraph: Another result of job satisfaction is improved attendance.

> The fourth paragraph describes a study tracking hundreds of employees who evaluated their level of job satisfaction. Low satisfaction correlated significantly with higher absenteeism and tardiness.

Transition sentence to concluding paragraph: Ultimately, splitting professional jobs makes sense.

> The concluding paragraph wraps up the argument that restructuring professional jobs into part-time positions can improve productivity, work quality, and attendance rates.

Many words and phrases help make transitions smooth. Most are phrases that point the reader forward to the next idea.

Common Transitional Words and Phrases

similarly	In the meantime
beyond	After a while
meanwhile	On the contrary
ultimately	In contrast to
subsequently	At the same time
therefore	Equally important
finally	In addition
moreover	In the future
also	To sum up
first	On the whole
second	In other words
third	For example

Exercise 3

Insert appropriate transitional words or phrases in the blanks that follow.

(1) _____ part-time workers typically are more productive per hour than their full-time colleagues, most employers are reluctant to hire part-time staff.

(2) _____, many employers limit career advancement for the few who manage to negotiate part-time contracts. There are several reasons this posture damages companies.

(3) _____, it is better to have several people under your roof who know a job rather than just one, who might quit and take away important information that no one else has.

(4) _____, part-timers usually are willing to negotiate minimal or reasonable benefits packages,

(5) _____ full-timers whose benefits can total over 35 percent of their salaries.

(6) _____, part-timers often pay a flexible employer back with unusually high morale and hard work. Full-timers,

(7) _____, often get burned out by the relentless demands of jobs that do not accomodate family or educational demands.

(8) _____, employers could gain great benefits by experimenting more with job sharing and new work schedule arrangements.

Sample solution appears on page 76.

Chapter Checkpoints

Paragraph Pointers

✓ One idea = one paragraph.

✓ Link paragraphs with clear transition sentences.

✓ Become comfortable with good transition phrases.

✓ Hone your topic sentences.

- Give shape and focus to your paragraphs.
- Capture the reader's attention.
- Give yourself a starting point.

✓ Avoid one sentence paragraphs, but keep them brief.

CHAPTER

3 | Getting Past the Blank Page

This chapter will help you to:

- Develop starting-out strategies like:

  Picking optimal work times and places.
  Visualizing the whole job before you start.
  Using traditional outlining.
  Brainstorming.
  Self-interviewing.
  Using the filling-in-the-form method.

- Learn when to use stuck-in-the-middle strategies like:

  Walking away from it all.

"Would you write a first draft of a thank-you letter for me?" Jackie Leone's supervisor asked. "It should take you only 10 minutes or so."

Jackie knew that this was not exactly true. The last time Jackie was given one of these "10-minute" jobs, it took her much longer. In this case, it took her over an hour to draft the thank-you letter. ■

Breakdown of Task	Time (in minutes)
Opening a file for the letter	1
Getting the return address and greeting set up	3
Proofreading the return address and greeting	2
Proofreading it again	1
Staring at the blank space	11

Breakdown of Task	Time (in minutes)
Going to get a cup of coffee	6
Proofreading the return address again	1
Feeling discouraged	9
Making a quick personal telephone call	7
Writing two sentences	10
Erasing one of the two sentences	1
Getting another cup of coffee	4
Writing the rest of the 10-line letter	19
Proofreading the letter	8
Printing	1

Total time on task: 1 hour, 24 minutes

How could Jackie have avoided wasting all this time? She could have used the starting-out strategies described in the following paragraphs.

STARTING-OUT STRATEGIES

Picking Optimal Work Times and Places

Little routines make your working time different from all other times of your day. Having a neat desk, your favorite coffee mug, or 10 minutes of meditation can affect whether it takes 10 minutes or 10 hours to get something done. Routines that signal concentration can save you a great deal of time if you develop and use them consistently.

Successful people protect and support their work habits. Their work areas fit their personalities and make them feel comfortable.

Very productive people often have an innate sense or have learned to schedule the hardest work for their most alert time of the day. If they have a slump right after lunch, they avoid scheduling demanding work after lunch. Productive people know what is easy for them and what is difficult, and they slot their most demanding work for the time when they can give it the most attention.

Not all of us have enough control over our workday to determine when or how we do our tasks. If more control over the flow of work would make you more efficient, it might be time to talk with your supervisor.

3

Visualizing the Whole Job Before You Start

Work expands to fill the time you have. If you are asked on Monday to write a short and simple report by Friday, you could spend the entire week completing the task which otherwise would have taken you a couple of hours at most to complete.

On Monday morning, Luis Paulo's boss, Amalia Samaraweera, asks him to write a short article on Jason Boxsworth, a new engineering employee, for the company's internal newsletter. Amalia asks Luis to complete the article by Friday.

Luis knows he will have to interview Jason to learn more about his professional background, his personal life, and his new role in the company. Luis also will need a copy of Jason's résumé.

In the past, articles like this have run about 200 words. Interviews have taken about 45 minutes. Luis knows he can get a résumé from the personnel department in 5 minutes if Jason does not have it on hand.

Luis knows what writing techniques work for him. He gets his ideas down on lots of Post-it™ self-stick notes and then arranges them on the wall in front of his desk until the article takes shape. Getting his notes done takes anywhere from 15 minutes to 4 hours, depending on the kind of writing job he is tackling. Writing an article, once he gets going, takes anywhere from 15 minutes to 3 days. When a job takes 3 days, typically 70% of this time is spent shuffling notes. The actual writing never takes more than 1 to 3 hours.

Luis looks at his assignment and sees the work breaking down as follows:

Task	Time (in minutes)	Percentage of Total Assignment
Interviewing	45	25
Getting ideas down on paper	25	14
Ordering ideas	30	17
Writing	60	33
Editing	20	11
Total time on assignment: 3 hours		

Seeing the job as a whole and dividing it into its parts helped Luis to keep the time he spent on this assignment under control. As a devoted Post-it note user, Luis put his task schedule on a large note and posted it beside his computer screen. This was a constant reminder to him that the assignment was totally under control.

Using Traditional Outlining

Some people's hearts sink when they hear the word *outline*. They can still smell the dust from their ninth-grade English classroom. The idea of squashing their work into neat *A*'s and *I*'s and little *a*'s is entirely unnatural to them.

There are good reasons to begin a writing task with an outline rather than to dive right in. Setting ideas in front of you on paper ensures that important points will not be forgotten.

Outlining also gives you a feeling of power that you cannot get when you try to juggle too many ideas in your mind. Some people who stall when faced with a blank page are simply feeling anxious about organizing what they have to say. As soon as words begin to appear on paper in an outline, control begins and anxiety fades.

The following exercise will help you understand the difficulty of juggling several ideas simultaneously if you are relying solely on your memory.

The ABC Exercise

1. Name all the possible combinations of the letters A, B, and C without using a pen and paper.
2. Name all the possible combinations of the letters A, B, C, and D without using a pen and paper.

Time each effort.

Now try both these exercises using pen and paper.

How did you do?

It is almost impossible to name the 24 combinations of the letters A, B, C, and D without notes. With a pen and paper most people can list them easily.

Our brains have limitations: all of us can examine both combinations of A and B. Only about one in four or five adults can give all six combinations of A, B, and C. Practically no one can recite the 24 possible combinations of A, B, C, and D.

Exercise 1

The Private Industry Council (PIC) has approached your company and asked that you offer summer jobs to 50 inner-city students who have never worked in a professional office setting. Your superior is not sure whether to say "yes" or "no." He has not had much experience with young employees and is nervous about a relationship with an unfamiliar nonprofit organization. He asks you to write a report that discusses the request and recommends a response to the PIC.

These are the ideas that run through your mind as you consider this assignment:

mailroom clerk typist

learning responsibility

time devoted to training summer staff

gaining exposure to professionals and professional job tracks

disciplining/managing young employees

scheduling complications

substituting for employees on vacation

janitor

public relations

earning money for college

developing references

mentors

file clerk

employee response to the hiring—anxiety, resentment of extra responsibility?

employee response to the hiring—fresh, interesting challenge?

dress codes

community service

training and identifying future employees

As you examine this random list, you begin to see that the items fall into categories:

1. How the program benefits the company, or: Why we need the program.
2. How the program benefits the students, or: Benefits of the program to participants.
3. Kinds of work students can do, or: Action plan; or Departments and divisions most likely to participate.

4. Obstacles, barriers, prejudices—things to overcome, or: Problem statement.

Move the items from your list into the four categories that you have identified.

1. How the program benefits the company.

    a. _____
    b. _____
    c. _____
    d. _____

2. How the program benefits the students.

    a. _____
    b. _____
    c. _____
    d. _____
    e. _____

3. Kinds of work students can do.

    a. _____
    b. _____
    c. _____
    d. _____

4. Obstacles, barriers, prejudices—things to overcome.

    a. _____
    b. _____
    c. _____
    d. _____
    e. _____

The solutions appear on pages 76 and 77.

Exercise 1 illustrates how to begin a traditional outline. Some writers could move directly from a rough outline like this to writing their memo or report. Others would need to embellish this outline. They would proceed to break down their ideas into subcategories and work out all their transition sentences, their introduction, and their conclusion before writing the memo or report.

Despite the usefulness of traditional outlining, some people cannot manage to write from a formal list. There is no rule that says you must outline or prepare your writing in any particular way.

If you can't work from an outline, you might try another method of organization. Here are a few alternatives to the traditional outline method.

Brainstorming

If outlines simply do not work for you, don't use them. Other methods may help you get started.

Just Write.   Sit down with a paper and pen (or in front of a computer screen) and record whatever runs through your head. When you feel you have written as much as you can, read what you have written. Cut out anything that is not relevant. Rearrange what is relevant so that related parts are together.

Set your work aside. Come back in half an hour, or half a day if you have more time, and reexamine your writing. Is your main point clearly explained? Have you supported this point with details? Set them in order. Do you have a conclusion? Draft one if you do not. Chop out anything you don't need.

This technique is not useful for all kinds of writers and situations. If you overwrite and don't eliminate extraneous information, this method might not be best for you. As a technique, this method reminds you that much of writing involves sitting, waiting, and churning out words. For some people the only way to get started is to roll along without a critical editing eye looking over their shoulder.

If intrusive editorial thoughts stop your "free" writing cold, consider creating a document spider or other visual aid.

Create a Document Spider.   A document spider is a graphic way to record your ideas. Ask yourself the following questions:

Why am I writing?

What point am I proving?

How do I want to persuade my reader?

What information am I transmitting?

Write your purpose in the middle of a circle. The points you want to make about this subject become the arms extending from the circle. Details supporting your points become branches of those arms.

Your spider does not have to be pretty, neat, or orderly. It can be merely lines and circles. Using the facts from Exercise 1 (earlier in this chapter), you can create a document spider that looks like this:

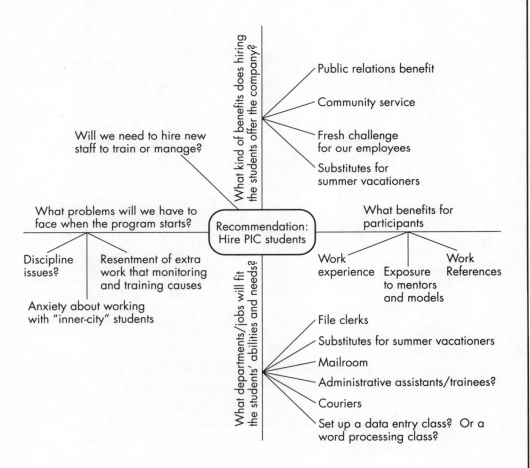

Create a Tree.   If it is easier to imagine parts of an argument, request, or report as parts of a tree, organize your ideas in the shape of a tree. Your main idea could function as the central trunk, and the supporting points could function as limbs. The facts from Exercise 1 could be laid out to look like a tree.

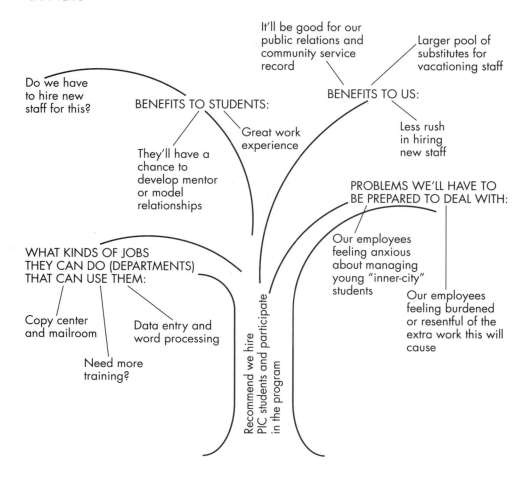

Fix Yourself a Hamburger!   If lines and lines of words intimidate you or slow you down, put some other image in your head.

Imagine a fast-food hamburger. The top and bottom buns become introductory and concluding paragraphs; the patties become supporting points.

If you like the idea of using images, find an image that is appropriate to the document you are writing and the kind of writer you are. The image may be a hamburger, a tree, a spider, or a chest of drawers. Keep in mind, however, that some writers hate the thought of creating images. To some, thinking in terms of hamburgers and trees feels uncomfortable and unhelpful. If images work for you, use them; if not, don't impose them on yourself.

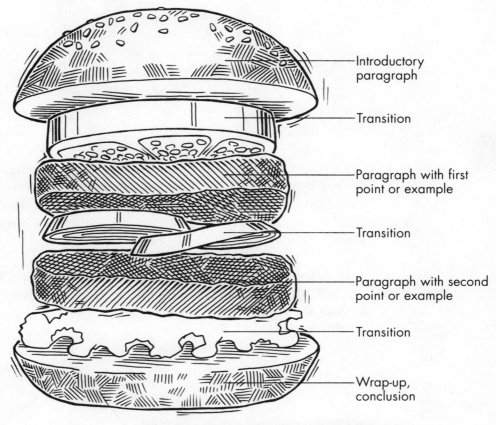

Introductory paragraph

Transition

Paragraph with first point or example

Transition

Paragraph with second point or example

Transition

Wrap-up, conclusion

THE HAMBURGER LETTER/MEMO OUTLINE

Exercise 2

You just got a new boss, and she has asked you to draft a description of your job. She is considering some personnel shifts, and you are eager to make her understand the value of your particular role. You dislike some aspects of your job and think they get in the way of accomplishing what is really important. You understand that this memo could change the nature of your job.

In the space below, use one of the start-up methods we have discussed to begin this memo.

_____
_____
_____
_____

_____
_____
_____
_____
_____
_____

Self-interviewing

Many of us have trouble starting to write for the simple reason that we are not ready to start. We have not asked ourselves the questions we need to get down to work. Or we have a vague idea of what we want to say, but we have not worked out the details. We cannot record our ideas until we have a clear focus.

If this is your situation, there are some very standard questions you can ask yourself about almost any kind of writing assignment. If you can answer them, most of your work is done. If you cannot, you will have trouble getting started.

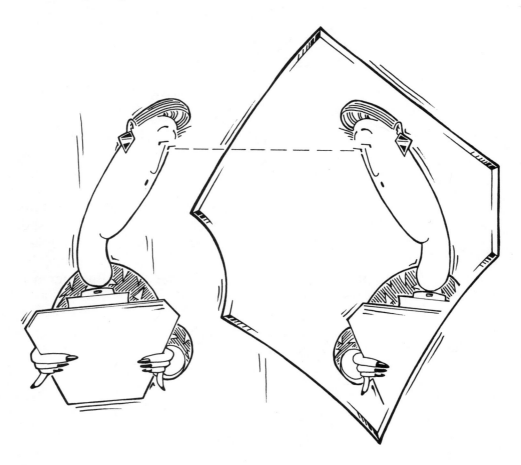

Consider the following questions as you begin. If you cannot answer them quickly, you'll need time to give them serious thought.

1. **Why am I writing this?** The answer to this question is the single most important thing to keep in mind as you write and edit. If you can identify your purpose, your hardest work may be done. Whether it is a letter, a memo, a newsletter article, a report, a proposal, or a speech, you must have its purpose in mind at all times. Is the document supposed to:

   Explain.

   Persuade.

   Thank.

   Request.

   Analyze.

   Report.

   Remember: If any line in your final document does not further your purpose, cut it out.

2. **What do you want your reader to think that he or she did not think before reading your letter, memo, or report?** For example, if you want your boss to allocate department funds to buy expensive software, by the time he's finished your memo on the subject you want him to pick up the telephone and order it because he sees how necessary or valuable the software is. Similarly, if you're setting up a meeting, you want the people who read your memo to think the agenda and the people involved are important enough to make attendance a priority. Always keep your end goal in mind as you work.

3. **What do you have to say to your reader to get the desired result?** What was it about that software that made you want it? Line these qualities up and set them down on paper. What could motivate someone to cancel another date to go to your lunch meeting? Whatever the reason, describe it at the beginning of your memo. This question is a good check on your own logic. If you have not done your homework on the software, for example, you will have difficulty describing the features that make it valuable to you. Some people find out at this stage of the game that the

3

software (or vendor, or equipment) that they thought they needed really is not what they want. Nothing clears the mind as well as having to explain something to another person.

4. **For whom are you writing?** Put yourself in your reader's position. Your boss probably has not been thinking about software for your job. Your colleagues might not be as eager as you are to come to a meeting whose subject is your job's priority, not theirs. Your boss is concerned about your productivity because it reflects on his or her supervisory skills. Therefore, software that increases your productivity is valuable. Your colleagues might not be as concerned about the meeting topic as you are, but if you make it clear that their input will shape a policy affecting their work lives, they will understand the meeting's importance. Knowing your reader also shapes the tone and content of documents. An internal memo to a subordinate will be very different from a letter going out to dozens of people who do not know you.

Filling-in-the-Form Method

If you have trouble interviewing yourself and are more comfortable with activities like filling in forms, then the filling-in-the-form method might be ideal for you.

This particular method—answering standard questions on a kind of form—works best for long pieces. It might be useful if you have to write an article for a newsletter, a report recommending some action, or a report on a project's progress.

To try this method, fill in the following form. It contains a series of questions with blank rules after them; it can be used as a standard form to be filled in at the beginning of your work.

The filled-in form represents the beginning of an outline. Now you can proceed to the document itself, or you can continue to fill in more details.

STUCK-IN-THE-MIDDLE STRATEGIES

Sometimes nothing works. You wade into the middle of a memo and just grind to a halt. You cannot come up with an outline, an idea, or answers to standard beginning questions. The simplest memo seems impossible.

Purpose of the document: _____
_____
_____

Points that will persuade or inform your reader:
    Point a: _____
    _____

    Point b: _____
    _____

    Point c: _____
    _____
    _____

Wrap-up statement: _____
_____
_____

3

For Simple Memos and Letters

Studies tell us that people who do not take regular breaks are less productive than those who do. If you have been frustrated by the same image on your screen for 15 minutes, it is time to change strategies.

Find a way to break out of that helpless feeling. You need to impose change. Here are some ways to do it:

1. Leave your office for a brisk, five-minute walk.
2. Have some toy stashed in your top drawer—juggling balls, a puzzle, a little basketball hoop and ball. Take a five-minute play-break.
3. Close your eyes and visualize a place in which you are perfectly happy. Once you get there, stay put for at least three minutes.

Now come back and face that blank page.

For More Complex Documents

1. **Stand up and walk away from your desk. Glance around. Flip through magazines and stop when some image catches your eye. Look out windows and over your colleagues' desks. Do this for five minutes.**

2. **Now pick up a pen and a piece of paper (sit down beside your desk) and list all the objects that caught your attention—what you saw in the magazine, or out the window, or on the desk.**

3. **Look at your list. Are there any common threads to it? Perhaps you will see a common mood. Or everything you chose might be the same color or size. In some cases your common threads might reflect back on the document you stepped away from.**

4. **Go back to your work, bringing your new observations about what was on your mind (or not on your mind) when you got stuck.**

Elaine Hoover is a mailroom supervisor. She is troubled that her peers in other mailrooms managed by her company have different standards for acceptable levels of employee error.

She discovers this when an employee from another site is transferred to her mailroom. The employee complains that Elaine's policy of giving someone an unpaid suspension after a third filing error is much too strict.

Elaine tells her boss, Margo Lustig, that the company should have the same standards at each site. Margo replies, "You're right. We should do that. What do you think the standards should be? Write me a memo."

Elaine asks around and discovers that, indeed, her mailroom has the toughest standards in the city. Are they too harsh? What does she think now that she knows her standards are different from the others? She plunges right into the memo, describing her own site's rules, and then finds that she is unsure of her thoughts. At first she tried to justify her own standards, then she tried to modify them to better match other supervisors' standards. Elaine got confused and stopped writing.

Elaine could not finish the memo. After 15 minutes of frustration, she walked away from her desk. She wandered around, noting the brass number on the building across the street, the list of numbers on a memo on her manager's desk, the logbook for incoming faxes, the graphs in an advertisement in a technical magazine.

3

Then she sat down and recorded everything that had caught her eye: the street number, the list on the memo, the logbook noting times on incoming faxes, the graphs. What did these things have in common? What could they tell her about the way she was approaching this problem?

Numbers. Everywhere she had looked she had been drawn to hard quantifiers. Perhaps this was her strength, her major interest, and the key to how she should look at this problem.

Elaine picked up the telephone and started making calls. "What are your absentee-ism rates?" she asked other supervisors in other sites. "How many minutes does it take on your site to get a fax or mail from your mailroom to the recipient? What's your error rate?"

Elaine realized that she was constructing an argument for her personnel policies out of numbers. Not only did her site have the best documented client service, but her staff's absenteeism rates were the lowest. She was not making her employees miserable with her standards; she was making them the best employees in the city. Elaine decided that she could establish a clear link between her standards and her results.

Elaine's earlier doubts about her standards vanished as she found her argument. Elaine reflected: "At a conscious level I'm not even aware of how many decisions I've made based on number results and how many systems I've set up that are number-driven. But that's my nature. I look at numbers first, always. And for figuring out if a system that counts minutes and pieces of mail works, there really isn't any substitute for them. I should have trusted my own instincts right from the start, except that I didn't recognize my instincts!" ■

Custom and habit or a temporary lack of confidence can stop you dead in your tracks as you tackle a new writing assignment. When you shift the spotlight off yourself and the frustration you feel at the moment and onto a random magazine illustration, for example, you may free yourself to continue thinking about the problem in a less conscious—and sometimes more productive—way. Does this method always work? To one degree or another it does. Even if it does not lead you directly to your best argument, it at least offers you an opportunity to interrupt unproductive moods or thought patterns. In ideal circumstances, it can help you jump over what is obstructing you.

Chapter Checkpoints

Break that Block

✓ Personalize your writer's block strategy—not every technique works for everyone. Experiment until you find one that gets you going.

✓ Set up a comfortable and familiar work space.

✓ Find your most productive time of day and do your most concentration-intensive work at that time.

✓ Visualize the whole job before you begin.

- What are its parts?
- How long will it take to conclude each part?
- How should I prioritize the component parts?
- Is there any way to avoid duplication of effort?

✓ Find a start-up method and use it consistently.

✓ How you start doesn't matter—it matters that you start.

4 | Organizing What You Have to Say

This chapter will help you to:

- Use mechanical organizing techniques.
- Decide how to order your material.

Li Wang was asked often to draft short reports for his boss. He had no problem getting started. He could sit and write down hundreds of ideas very quickly. Notes and relevant articles would be scattered all over his desk.

Li's problem was moving beyond the start-up process and *writing* the report. He usually ended up buried in a mass of notes, with a vague idea of what his main point would be but with no clear structure to organize his notes into a final report. So he gathered more and more information, talked to more and more people, and made more and more notes. But he never finished his reports. ■

MECHANICAL ORGANIZING TECHNIQUES

Li Wang could have used several techniques to help him move from his pile of notes to actually writing his report. A description of these techniques follows.

Post-it Notes

You can put your ideas and points on Post-it notes. Stick them all over your wall and arrange them according to topic and importance. You quickly will see where you need more detail and what you need to put aside.

When you first start putting ideas on the post-it notes, don't edit yourself.

Put down anything that occurs to you. Just getting your ideas flowing is what is critical.

If you are a writer who gets bogged down at this stage of the writing process, decide how many minutes you will allow yourself to "start up"; when those minutes have elasped, shift gears and start to edit and analyze what you have written.

An illustration of how Post-it notes might speed up the process of organizing your ideas is shown on the facing page.

Index Cards

Index cards can be used the same way as Post-it notes. Lay out the index cards, each containing a point that you need to address in your document, next to one another on a flat surface so you can see them as a coherent group of related ideas. Then prioritize and group the cards.

Headlines

If you have trouble shaping a memo or report, try using bold headlines. Headlines act as abbreviated topic sentences, giving the reader a quick overview of the contents of your report or memo.

Headlines are tailored to fit the individual document, so there are no standard ones for all situations. Think of headlines as a listing of the ideas your reader must know or consider.

Be willing to tailor the headlines of a report or memo to the situation. A progress report for a job that is going smoothly, for example, will have different headlines than a report for a job that is not going well. Despite individual differences, however, some patterns do exist. Some common subject areas for headlines are given on page 48.

The wall after 30 minutes:

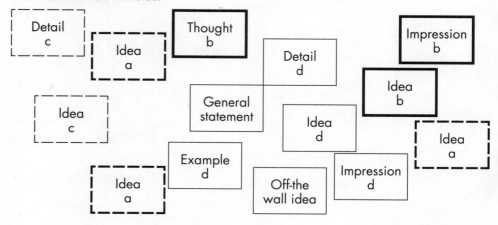

The wall after 45 minutes:

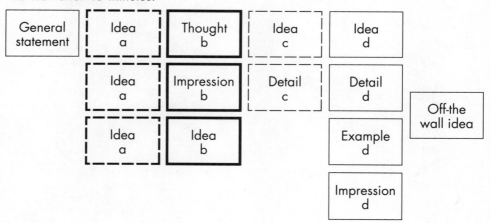

The wall after one hour:

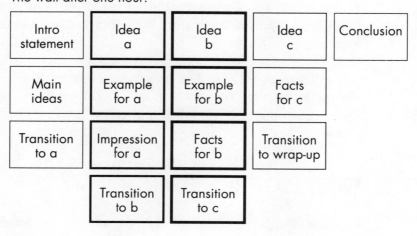

4

4

Kind of Document	Subject Areas That Get Headlined
Progress Report	Background information Problem statement Achievements to date a. in chronological order b. in order of importance c. in order of responsible division/people Remaining tasks Budget details/information, if pertinent Recommendations for action/changes Summary
Procedural Change Report	Background information Rationale for making changes in procedure Recommended change Repercussions of change Implementation issues Summary
Work Order	Work description Rationale Responsible division (or, if an outside vendor is needed, necessary qualities of vendor) Timeline Budget
Recommendation Report	Problem description Recommended solution(s) Rationale Action plan Predicted challenges Summary
Meeting Announcement	Time and place Involved personnel Purpose of meeting Preparation (if any) for meeting Follow up actions requested (if any)

These headlines can act as starting points for your outline, and remain in the final report as organizing signposts. Put them in boldface or a larger font.

The following is the start of a memo being organized with headlines. The writer sets the headlines in bold and then fills in the blanks beneath them, returning later to polish and edit a final version.

WORKING FROM START-UP NOTES

In Chapter 3 we considered various ways to get started, including just writing and using visual aids as ways of brainstorming your ideas on paper. These methods are a first step in the organizational process.

To: Li Wang
From: Yolanda Littlejohn
Re: Finding a new paper supplier
Date: June 17, 1993

Why we need to switch suppliers

Fill in with paragraphs describing current problems and needs. These might be:

Problems with our current supplier:

Specific materials and services that we do need:

Possible new suppliers

Offer researched information about suppliers giving each a subheading:

First Possible Supplier

    Prices

    Services

    Available materials

Second Possible Supplier

    Prices

    Services

    Available materials

Third Possible Supplier

    Prices

    Services

    Available materials

My recommendation

Conclude with recommendation for a new supplier, with rationale for the choice.

With the document spider, after the arms are in place, you can begin to assess your progress. Which arms of information are most important? Which are least important? What have you left out, and what should you add?

When you edit start-up notes like the document spider, do not get

4

unnerved by the mess. You often will find new ideas pop up or that the way you originally saw addressing the problem does not work anymore.

Mid-organizational confusion is normal—even good. It usually is a sign you really are thinking about the issue in a fresh way, without preconceptions, or prejudices. You are open to new perspectives and are struggling to see the whole problem as it is—not as the neat outline you pictured before you got down to work.

The following illustration is the document spider started in Chapter 3. The spider has been marked up by an organizing writer. You will see that the writer has:

1. Identified related ideas by drawing circles around them.
2. Numbered the cricles in order of importance—the order in which they will appear in the document.
3. Crossed out ideas that should not reach the final document (circle 6).
4. Scanned the page for repeated ideas (substitutes for summer

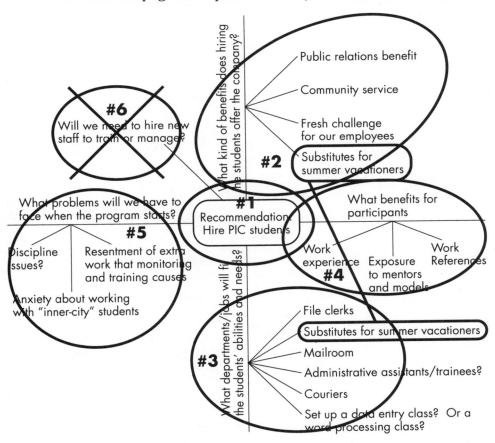

vacations) or ideas that appear in more than one section that are closely related. Attention is drawn to such repetitions graphically. The writer will have to evaluate these kinds of occurrences and decide where each idea should go.

Each of the circles in the spider represents a section of your final document. Depending upon the final document's length and detail, each circle could end up as a single paragraph or as several paragraphs. In this particular spider diagram, the sections are numbered according to their importance.

ORDERING THE PARTS

Order by Importance

Ordering according to importance is probably the most common way to organize business documents. The reason is very simple—the writer wants to begin with his most critical idea. This ensures that:

- The reader will not be misled or confused about the document's purpose.
- The busy reader will get the most important information, even if he or she cannot read every word.
- The busy reader will know immediately whether this document must be read.

In a memo recommending that a company participate in the Private Industry Council's (PIC) summer hiring program (from Chapter 3), the writer would order what he or she has to say as follows:

1. Thesis statement paragraph recommending company participation.
2. Strongest defense of the opinion, describing benefits to the company if it participates.
3. Second strongest defense, describing benefits to the hired students.
4. Description of where the students would fit in the company and what kinds of jobs they could do.
5. Paragraph positioned at the end to address unpleasant problems that could pop up as the hiring for the program begins.
6. Concluding paragraph, restating the position.

The order of this memo displays the information the reader wants right up front—the answer to the question, what should we do? It then defends the recommendation with a "why" statement. Just as important, it anticipates questions and resistance by acknowledging them and treating them as manageable situations.

Order by Chronology

Work plans, explanations of complex series of incidents, instructions on how to do a task or follow a procedure—these are examples of writing tasks that are best ordered chronologically.

This technique can be used in many situations. Here is how it might look when applied to our PIC program:

To: Sharon Elliot, Vice President in Charge of Community Relations
From: José Bernstein, Human Resources
Re: Participation in PIC Summer Jobs Program
Date: June 2, 1993

We have been asked to respond to the PIC's request that we participate in their summer hiring program. I believe that we should participate.

If we proceed, I recommend the following steps:

Date	Action
June 1993	▪ Screen potential student hires. ▪ Meet with participating department heads to explain the program. ▪ Run small group sessions with employees to help them understand program goals and to air concerns. ▪ Select and match mentors. ▪ Hold press conference to announce the program publicly and explain our involvement.
July 1993	▪ Place new hires in the mailroom, the copy center, data entry, or word processing. ▪ Mentors meet with their students weekly.
August 1993	▪ Evaluate student performance.
September 1993	▪ Meet with PIC staff to evaluate program and modify as needed. ▪ Release reports on program success to press. ▪ Make job offers, if appropriate, to successful seniors who participated in the summer program.

May 1994	▪ Begin department training and focus groups to prepare our own employees for the program.
	▪ Hold press conference, involving community leaders and students if possible.
June 1994	▪ Match students with mentors and jobs.
July 1994	▪ Students begin work and meet weekly with mentors.
August 1994	▪ Program continues.
September 1994	▪ Wrap-up reports and evaluation meeting with PIC staff and involved company staff.
	▪ Release data and stories to press.

Order by Sequence

Ordering by sequence is a particularly good method for instructions, work plans, and other communications that demand step-by-step explanation. A sequentially organized report related to the PIC program might look something like this:

Instructions to Mentors Working with PIC Hires

1. Attend training sessions for mentors to get better idea of what to expect and what duties are involved.
2. Hold an initial meeting with your student during the second week of July and each week thereafter for the rest of his or her employment here.
3. Advise students on work issues, help them understand company procedures, and, if necessary, act as their intermediaries and advocates with their supervisors.
4. Work with students' immediate supervisors to draft evaluation of their work.
5. Complete final program report and submit to Personnel.

Order by Persuasion

If you are making a point, stating a conclusion, or arguing an opinion, you must decide whether to begin with your conclusion. In most cases you should. If you think your company should install a time clock, for example, the fastest way to convince someone of your position is to come right out and say what you think.

There is an exception to this general rule, however. Assume that a time clock is a very controversial idea in your company. Many people reading your memo believe a time clock is an insult to employees and an unnecessary control. When you must state an unpopular opinion or state something that your reader might immediately dismiss, order your material so your reader will have to pay attention to your supporting facts before dismissing your conclusion. In this case, state your conclusion last.

The following diagram illustrates how you might organize your memo on time clocks when you expect a hostile reaction:

We have no formal system to recognize many of the ways that some employees are more responsible than others.

It is not fair to prompt and responsible employees to allow other employees to be chronically late.

Our company could benefit from a system that measured, identified, and rewarded responsible employee behavior.

We could increase productivity by increasing accountability.

Time clocks could accomplish this for us.

What if the situation were different and the memo were going from a supervisor who wanted time clocks to a manager who liked the idea but was concerned about how unhappy the move might make employees? In this case, the memo might be organized with its conclusion right up front.

We should install
a time clock.

Some of our employees are
chronically late, and it is not fair
to prompt employees who work
longer hours for the same pay.

Our company could benefit from a system
that measured, identified, and rewarded
responsible employee behavior.

We could increase productivity by
increasing accountability.

Ultimately, all employees would be happier
working in a more fair and profitable environment.

Order by Comparison

Comparing different positions is yet another way to organize material. Suppose that you are comparing A and B. You can organize a report or memo by alternating paragraphs on A with paragraphs on B. Categories of comparison might be distinguished by bold headlines. If A were *we should hire PIC students* and B were *we should not hire PIC students*, your memo might look like this:

First paragraph:	How the company could benefit from hiring PIC students
Second paragraph:	Possible opposition to this plan
Third paragraph:	Solutions to the opposition

Fourth paragraph: How students and employees would benefit from the program

Concluding paragraph: We should hire

Order by Spatial Organization

In some situations, the most effective way to organize material is spatially. For example, if you are describing a complex tool, you can describe its parts based on how they actually are attached to each other, starting from the left and working to the right. You would show the parts as they exist spatially, one after the other.

■ Exercise 1

Helen Spencer works for a company that provides copy services to corporations. Helen's company actually sets up a copy center in its clients' offices, brings in the equipment and staff, and runs the center.

Helen runs a copy center in an insurance company, and she is in trouble. Francis Jessup, the insurance company administrator, has told Helen that he is extremely unhappy because Helen's company promised him that there would be five people covering the copy machines. The last two times Francis entered the copy center only three people were visible. Helen knows that one of the missing employees was sick and the other was hand-delivering emergency jobs to people who had gotten them in at the last minute.

Helen also knows that she has never missed a deadline and that she maintains very good quality control over her center's work. She is adequately staffed, but she has to prove this to the client.

"Your contract ends in two months, and I'm opening this job to other vendors for bid. You'd better get together a proposal for me, because I'm not so sure that you're the best company to run our copy center," Francis tells her. ■

A

Report on recent
study on customer
satisfaction level

_____
_____
_____
_____
_____
_____

B

Equipment
analysis

_____
_____
_____
_____
_____
_____

C

Background:
Description of current
services

_____
_____
_____
_____
_____

D

Proposal
to
Alamo Insurance
Company
from
Ajax
Copies

E

Projected work
volume

_____
_____
_____
_____
_____

F

Contents

_____

_____

_____

G

Proposed changes
from current
services

_____
_____
_____
_____
_____
_____

H

Estimate of costs
for services

_____
_____
_____
_____
_____
_____

I

Personnel: staffing,
training

_____
_____
_____
_____
_____
_____

J

Report
abstract

_____
_____
_____
_____
_____

K

Summary

_____
_____
_____
_____
_____
_____

L

Quality controls

_____
_____
_____
_____
_____
_____

4

Helen must sit down with her supervisor and write a proposal to the insurance company now, to convince the unhappy administrator that she and her staff do offer the best service at the most economical cost.

A draft of the proposal's layout is in random order. Refer to the pages by the letters that appear in the upper right-hand corner of each page. How should Helen order the pages for her final memo? Fill in the page letters next to the sequential numbers that appear below.

1. _____   7. _____

2. _____   8. _____

3. _____   9. _____

4. _____   10. _____

5. _____   11. _____

6. _____   12. _____

The solution appears on page 77.

Chapter Checkpoints

Organize that Document

✓ Organizational skills are learned through practice.

✓ Try different ways to get organized.

   Post-it notes.

   Index cards.

   Headlines.

   Traditional outlines.

✓ Base your organization on proven methods.

   By importance.

   By chronological order.

   By sequential order.

✓ Visualize your report or letter as a:

   Chart.

   Graph.

   Tree.

   Pyramid.

✓ Find an image that gives shape to your thoughts and use it to organize your ideas.

5 | Final Checks to Ensure Success

This chapter will help you to:

- Focus on the purpose of your document and the end results.
- Maintain a positive point of view.
- Focus on problems rather than personalities.
- Assume respect and goodwill among colleagues.

Several basic business attitudes can guide you as you write, speak, fax, or e-mail to your colleagues. These attitudes do not change from one kind of communication to another. They do not change from one decade to another.

KEEP YOUR EYE ON THE END RESULT

Whatever you are writing, use your purpose as your organizing principle. Do you want a manufacturer to refund your money? Do you want a subordinate to stop rolling in to work 10 minutes late?

Clearly ask for what you want. Never end a business communication requiring a response without actually stating what you want the reader to do.

This letter is an example of a poor end to a business communication.

June 10, 1993

Mr. Peter Ash, Manufacturer's Representative
Fabrics International
22 Warehouse Alley
Portland, ME 92842

Dear Peter:

We have been using your tent canvas for several years and until recently we were happy with what you delivered.

The last shipment of material we got from you, however, had several flaws. The colors were not consistent or vibrant and the final waterproof coating was not as effective as you claimed. Our quality control people tell us it leaks like a sieve when they do waterproofing checks. We cannot possibly use it for our tents unless we want to risk losing our own customers.

You know that we run on a tight schedule. Getting this bad canvas has meant that we cannot finish our tents and fill our own orders to sporting goods stores on time.

We feel you should respond to the problem immediately.

Sincerely,

Tom Post

This letter makes it clear that Tom and his colleagues are not happy with the material the manufacturer supplied them. It explains why. It gives detail. What is the manufacturer supposed to do about it? What does Tom want? Does he want his money back? Is he ending his relationship with the manufacturer? Does he want new material? Does he just want to complain?

If Tom does not directly tell Peter Ash what he wants, Peter will have a hard time pleasing Tom.

Here is another way Tom could have dealt with the problem.

In this letter, Tom makes it clear that he wants new material from the manufacturer by July 10. Tom states that if a problem prevents Peter Ash from doing what Tom wants, Peter should contact Tom immediately. Tom lets the manufacturer know the urgency of the response time, but his tone is not hysterical or blaming.

Tom includes a subject line so that there is no doubt about what the letter addresses. He places the order number in the subject line so that the paper trail on his order can be traced quickly. He makes it as easy for the manufacturer as he can.

June 10, 1993

Mr. Peter Ash, Manufacturer's Representative
Fabrics International
22 Warehouse Alley
Portland, ME 92842

SUBJECT: Request for free replacement of defective material purchased March 13, 1992, Order # LI82729

Dear Peter:

I write to report some problems with the last shipment of material we ordered from you and to ask that your company replace the defective goods.

The last shipment of material had several flaws. The colors were not consistent or vibrant. When our quality control people tested it they found that the final waterproof coating was not effective.

We know that this is not the norm for your tent material, which deserves its reputation as the best on the market. We assume you will be as anxious to correct this flaw as we are.

In the meantime, we are now behind schedule in tent production because we cannot proceed with the material you sent us. We feel confident that you will replace order # LI82729 with nondefective material no later than July 10.

If you cannot respond to our request and deadline, please contact me immediately.

Thank you for your prompt response. We look forward to receiving the new material.

Sincerely,

Tom Post

5

Tom is very likely to get what he wants—a fast replacement for the defective shipment. He also gets a grateful supplier who will bend over backward for him in the future because he did not cancel his account at the first tough juncture in their relationship. Tom is using this problem to build strong business ties.

THE POSITIVE POINT OF VIEW

Tom's positive tone is as important to his letter as its content. He makes sure that Peter Ash knows that he respects the manufacturer's work ("We know that this is not the norm for your tent material, which deserves its reputation as the best on the market."). More important, he lets Peter know that he is confident that they agree on the problem's urgency ("We assume you will be as anxious to correct this flaw as we are."). Tom's tone is assured, professional, and positive. It assumes that there is no difficulty that cannot be overcome.

Why is a positive tone so hard to achieve? Because in the push and shove of daily work, particularly work that is deadline-sensitive or work that is not going well, people feel anxious and defensive. They make the critical mistake of conveying these feelings to their readers. The communicator who passes on anxiety and blame generates anxiety and defensiveness. Anxious, defensive people do not do their best work. They cannot respond, and they cannot help you deal with your problems.

FOCUS ON THE PROBLEM, NOT THE PERSON

A good last check on any business communication is a quick search for "I" and "you." If you find more than one sentence beginning with "you," evaluate all of your sentences for tone. Have you shifted your attention to a person rather than the work at hand?

What kind of a response would Tom have gotten had he written the following letter?

June 10, 1993

Mr. Peter Ash, Manufacturer's Representative
Fabrics International
22 Warehouse Alley
Portland, ME 92842

SUBJECT: Request for free replacement of defective material purchased March 13, 1992, Order # LI82729

Dear Peter:

Your last shipment to us was defective, and I write to ask you to replace the order and do something about your poor materials and irresponsible quality control.

Your people could not possibly have checked for waterproofing or color, since both were defective. You did not catch the problem and then you went ahead and shipped it off to us.

Your carelessness has jeopardized our own relationships with the sporting goods stores that are waiting for the tents that we cannot make because of problems in your product.

I assume you will ship us a new, more carefully inspected replacement by July 10. If you cannot do this, please contact me immediately.

Thank you for your prompt response. We look forward to receiving the new material.

Sincerely,

Tom Post

All the same points are made—the specific problems, the repercussions, the request for a replacement within a specified time—but the tone is very different.

Most poeple in Peter Ash's chair, reading this letter, would realize that Tom's problem is valid and requires attention. They would realize that Tom is not personally angry with *them* but is angry about the condition of the material. Yet, the tone of this letter feels personal. Angry letters that feel personal tend to generate self-protective rather than productive responses.

If Peter Ash received this letter from Tom, his first concern might not be to solve the problem. It might be to protect his personal reputation and to vent a little anger at this person who seems furious with him.

Exercise 1

Assume that you are Susan Fairweather's supervisor and that she is consistently 10 minutes late to work. Draft two memos to Joanna, the first an example of a blaming, person-centered, negative approach; the second a problem-centered, positive statement of what you need from her.

Memo One

To: Susan Fairweather
From:
Re:
Date:

_____
_____
_____
_____
_____
_____
_____
_____
_____
_____
_____
_____
_____
_____
_____
_____
_____
_____
_____
_____
_____
_____
_____
_____
_____
_____
_____
_____
_____
_____
_____
_____
_____
_____
_____
_____

A sample solution appears on page 78.

Memo Two

To: Susan Fairweather
From:
Re:
Date:

_____
_____
_____
_____
_____
_____
_____
_____
_____
_____
_____
_____
_____
_____
_____
_____
_____
_____
_____
_____
_____
_____
_____
_____
_____
_____
_____
_____
_____
_____
_____
_____
_____

A sample solution appears on page 78.

RESPECT AND GOODWILL AMONG COLLEAGUES

In Chapter 1, we learned that people often "mirror" the behavior that is directed at them. If they are treated with respect, they treat their colleagues accordingly.

This is a basic tenet of successful communication and one of the hardest to follow. Ultimately, however, it is worth the effort because:

1. It improves the quality of everyday work life.
2. It builds productive and trusting work relationships.
3. It creates a work climate in which mistakes and problems can be honestly faced (and therefore solved).

This attitude is reflected in actual business writing through:

1. The steady use of the active voice.
2. The reliable use of facts and details, without evasions.
3. Little or no use of unnecessary, "padding" language.

In short, problems are not hidden or avoided. They are faced. Facing problems means holding people responsible for the quality of their work. Respect and goodwill do not preclude holding individuals to the standards of their job. In fact, they demand it.

Chapter Checkpoints

Communication Is Key

✓ Stick to your purpose—keep your messages direct and clear.

✓ Avoid negative, accusatory endings.

✓ Keep a positive point of view.

✓ Be careful not to put your reader on the defensive.

✓ Focus on problems, not personalities.

✓ Remember that you want to work *with* the reader, not prove a point or place blame.

✓ Assume respect and goodwill among colleagues.

Post-Test

This post-test is designed to reinforce the material you have read in this book. If you have difficulty with any question, refer back to the text for a quick review.

1. Clarify the following:

   at the present time   _____

   due to the fact that   _____

   in order that   _____

   with regard to   _____

   utilize   _____

   visualize   _____

   in the near future   _____

   ascertain   _____

   concur   _____

   facilitate   _____

   endeavor (as a verb)   _____

   in close proximity   _____

2. Identify two strengths that the active voice can give your writing.

   _____

   _____

3. Identify three specific strategies for quickly getting down to work as a writer.

   _____

   _____

   _____

4. How many ideas can a paragraph typically address gracefully?

   _____

5. Identify two characteristics of a successful, businesslike "tone."

   _____

   _____

6. Identify three techniques that help organize ideas on paper.

   _____

   _____

   _____

7. What is the most important question writers can ask themselves about the memo, report, or letter they are developing?

   _____

8. Identify two questions other than the one you cited in Question 7 that can guide a writer's work.

_____

_____

9. What specific steps can a writer take when stalled in the middle of a writing task?

_____

_____

_____

_____

10. Identify two specific techniques any writer can use to ensure that his or her letters or memos get the kinds of responses desired.

_____

_____

ANSWER KEY

1. Now; because; so; about; use; see; imagine; soon; learn; agree; make easier; try; near.
2. Maintains a brisk and controlled pace; makes your message clearer
3. Arrange your work space in ways that make you comfortable and signal that it is now time to work; visualize your entire task before beginning; break the task, if it is large, into smaller parts.
4. One.
5. Courtesy; brevity.
6. Outlining; brainstorming; creating spider or tree diagrams.
7. Why am I writing this?
8. Who is reading this? What must you say to your reader to get your desired result or reaction?
9. Step away from your desk; think about something else. If that doesn't help, note all the things that attract your attention, sit down again and examine what attracted your attention, and ask yourself if it throws any light on why you got stalled, or on how to continue your document. Change outlining techniques or strategies. Just write—do not edit or stop yourself. Conduct a self-interview to focus your purpose. Create a form that guides your thinking by asking you basic questions about your end and purpose.
10. Focus on the problem, not on personalities; maintain a positive tone. Other acceptable answers include: write clearly; write concisely; maintain a clear attitude of cooperation and respect.

Solutions to Exercises

Chapter One

Exercise 1 (page 3)

1. Janice wants to shorten time spent managing telemarketers. She also thinks they are not evaluated often enough.
2. I do not believe that the equipment was shipped on time. I also see that the invoicing was not coordinated with the ordering process.

Exercise 2 (page 4)

1. The management would like all employees to write clearly and simply.
2. The accident happened at the park near Route 5.
3. I have identified the memos that need legal review.
4. Hiring temporary help will make it possible to meet our deadline.
5. The computer cost $1,001.50.
6. I recommended that we redistribute accounts among managers after July 31.

Exercise 3 (page 6)

Wordy or Complex	Clearer
at the present time	now
due to the fact that	because
in order that	so that
with regard to	as to
utilize	use
visualize	see *or* imagine
in the near future	soon
ascertain	learn *or* understand
concur	agree
facilitate	help *or* make easier
endeavor (as a verb)	try
in close proximity	near
in view of the fact that	because of *or* due to

Exercise 4 (page 7)

1. The division director stated the problem.
2. We should avoid the problem.
3. We suggest that the finance department form a review board to oversee cash flow.
4. Increased sales over the last quarter will make bonuses a possibility this year.
5. He (or she) assigned positions without regard for previous experience and existing responsibilities.

Exercise 5 (page 10)

1. If your department meets deadlines, it will be regarded as highly successful.
2. We take telephone orders Monday through Friday, from 8 A.M. to 6 P.M.
3. People will pay as much as $150 for this product.
4. A great deal of our work is responding to customer complaints.
5. Timely advice and assistance can prevent errors from happening.

Exercise 6 (page 14)

January 12, 1993

Ms. Cassandra Epstein
Johnson Alarm Company
36th North Avenue
Natick, MA 02368

Dear Ms. Epstein:

We write to alert you to a problem with your product and ask for repair or replacement.

On December 3, 1992, we purchased three alarms from your company (Invoice No. 0287351) which have since been going off at random times. Obviously, this is not appropriate or safe.

Your company has an excellent reputation, based in good part on its responsiveness to customer need. That is one of the reasons we turned to you for the original purchase, and it is why we are confident now that you will repair or replace the system at no cost to us.

Could you please call us at 508-233-8000 to make arrangements? We look forward to hearing from you or your representative within the week.

Thank you for your attention.

Sincerely,

Harvey Diaz

Chapter Two

Exercise 1 (page 20)

I think that everyone needs an old-fashioned wife. Nothing is more comforting than walking in the door at the end of a long day and smelling a home-cooked meal in the oven. Everyone needs someone to set up their social calendar and get the car to the mechanic when it's on the fritz.

Good old-fashioned wives listen attentively to your stories, don't bore you with complaints about being a good old-fashioned wife, and raise children so polite and good-hearted that they let you eat dinner uninterrupted. If they work, they still get that dinner in the oven by the time you reach the door, and they hold jobs that let them stay home with the kids if they're sick and get there late because they had to get the car to the garage.

To sum up, if my husband would let me get married, I'd go looking for one tomorrow, but he's against it. So—I remain wifeless.

Exercise 2 (Page 21)

1. *All the frustrations of Andy's day left him feeling short-tempered and anxious.* The moment he arrived at work, he discovered three errors in the night shift's work. Worse, the errors attracted a great deal of attention because Andy's own boss chose this particular day to drop in and review the morning shipping schedule. Not only did everything seem to go wrong, but everyone in the world seemed to be watching it happen.

2. *The best way to handle paperwork is to touch each document that crosses your desk only once.* If a document is highly important, telephone, write, or dictate a response immediately. If it is moderately important, dash off a reply directly on the letter or memo itself, or redirect it to an appropriate person. If you believe it

could wait, let it wait—forever. Toss it in a special drawer that holds things you never expect to do. This is the most efficient use of your time.

3. You can be someone who works methodically, never leaving any detail to rest until your work seems perfect. You can be sweepingly quick, happier accomplishing a great deal than one perfect thing. You can be a dreamer who is concerned with nothing at all but what is in your head at any given moment. *You can succeed no matter what kind of person you are, if only you find a life's work that fits your character.*

4. *People typically do not think of prejudice in the workplace as something that extends to those with weight problems, but it does.* We know that women, the disabled, and minorities suffer job discrimination. But it is also true that individuals who are more than 20 pounds overweight are offered less money to do the same job as slender colleagues; in some cases the overweight are even rejected for jobs based on nothing but their physical appearance.

Exercise 3 (page 24)

1. Although
2. Moreover
3. First
4. Second
5. in contrast to
6. Third *or* Finally
7. on the other hand *or* however
8. To sum up *or* In conclusion

Chapter Three

Exercise 1 (page 31)

1. How the program benefits the company
   a. training and identifying future employees
   b. public relations
   c. community service
   d. employee response to the hiring—fresh, interesting challenge?
2. How the program benefits the kids
   a. learning responsibility

    b. developing references

    c. mentors

    d. earning money for college

    e. gaining exposure to professionals and professional job tracks

3. Kinds of work kids can do

    a. file clerk

    b. janitor

    c. mailroom clerk typist

    d. standing in for employees on vacation

4. Obstacles, barriers, prejudices—things to overcome

    a. dress codes

    b. time devoted to training summer staff

    c. scheduling complications

    d. disciplining/managing young employees

    e. employee response to the hiring—anxiety, resentment of extra responsibility?

Chapter Four

Exercise 1 (page 56)

This exercise has a few acceptable solutions. Sections such as "Report on recent study on customer satisfaction level" could appear at the beginning, middle, or end of the proposal—but in this case Helen knows that she has never missed a deadline and that customer satisfaction is high. She needs this fact to be right up front since her contact person is implying that her staffing is hurting the quality of service her company offers.

Francis specifically has questioned the number of people Helen has on the premises, so a section titled "Personnel: Staffing, Training" was included and placed before the discussion of equipment needs. If the client were concerned about adequacy of equipment, this order would have been reversed. Helen also knows her quality control systems are particularly good, so she invents and includes the section, "Quality Controls."

The section on "Background" typically is the first in a proposal, but Helen and her boss feel that it is important, given their vulnerable position, to establish the strength of their services before they review the extent of their services. The client already knows what they do—he is questioning how well they do it.

1. D	**7.** C
2. J	**8.** G
3. F	**9.** E
4. A	**10.** B
5. I	**11.** H
6. L	**12.** K

■ Chapter Five

Exercise 1 (page 66)

Keep in mind that these sample memos represent only one possible approach. Other solutions are acceptable as long as they use an appropriate tone.

MEMO ONE (BLAMING APPROACH)

To: Susan Fairweather
From: (Your Name)
Re: Irresponsible behavior
Date: August 19, 1993

You have fallen into a regular pattern of unprofessional behavior, and I write to warn you that if it continues, appropriate disciplinary steps will be taken. You cannot get to work 10 or 15 minutes late every day and expect that no one will notice. Everyone notices your irresponsible behavior, and you damage morale when you act like you can behave in ways that everyone knows are unacceptable.

You clearly are at fault and I advise you to change your behavior immediately.

MEMO TWO (PROBLEM-CENTERED APPROACH)

To: Susan Fairweather
From: (Your Name)
Re: Chronic lateness
Date: August 19, 1993

We both know that promptness is important for many reasons: it shows commitment to the job, it reflects a general sense of responsibility, and it shows respect for one's colleagues who also must get to work at the same time.

That is why I bring your attention to the fact that you have been at least 10 minutes late to work on 15 out of the last 25 workdays. Occasional lateness is unavoidable, but this has become a pattern that must be broken or you will face disciplinary action.

I am confident that you can be consistently prompt, and I expect to note significant improvement at your next job review, which is scheduled for mid-September.

THE BUSINESS SKILLS EXPRESS SERIES

This growing series of books addresses a broad range of key business skills and topics to meet the needs of employees, human resource departments, and training consultants.

To obtain information about these and other Business Skills Express books, please call Business One IRWIN toll free at: 1-800-634-3966.

Effective Performance Management	ISBN 1-55623-867-3
Hiring the Best	ISBN 1-55623-865-7
Writing that Works	ISBN 1-55623-856-8
Customer Service Excellence	ISBN 1-55623-969-6
Writing for Business Results	ISBN 1-55623-854-1
Powerful Presentation Skills	ISBN 1-55623-870-3
Meetings that Work	ISBN 1-55623-866-5
Effective Teamwork	ISBN 1-55623-880-0
Time Management	ISBN 1-55623-888-6
Assertiveness Skills	ISBN 1-55623-857-6
Motivation at Work	ISBN 1-55623-868-1
Overcoming Anxiety at Work	ISBN 1-55623-869-X
Positive Politics at Work	ISBN 1-55623-879-7
Telephone Skills at Work	ISBN 1-55623-858-4
Managing Conflict at Work	ISBN 1-55623-890-8
The New Supervisor: Skills for Success	ISBN 1-55623-762-6
The *Americans with Disabilities Act:* What Supervisors Need to Know	ISBN 1-55623-889-4